Honey Bees & Beekeeping
A Mental Health Miracle

D1713694

Disclaimer

Dedication

This book is dedicated to every kid who loves honey! It is also for every kid that has ever given unselfishly for the happiness and prosperity of another. To every person that loves the outdoors and understands that the answers to all can be

found in Mother Nature. Every person that appreciates the honey bee and all of the goods produced from their diligent labor. Every person who supports the preservation of the honey bee and also to those who recognize the honey bee's contribution to humanity, our health, and environment. This book is dedicated to my parents, grandmothers Me-Mal, and Bessa for the priceless

roles they've played and continue to play in my life, uncle Shawn for introducing me to the life of the honey bee and beekeeping; all of the seminars, workshops, and health benefits that have come from them. Lastly, this project is dedicated to every individual, program, organization, and charity that has donated their time, resources, and finances to help encourage me to continue promoting health and unity within our communities. You are greatly appreciated.

INTRODUCTION

So, you are thinking about keeping bees. I think it is excellent! I think our world will be much better off if everyone started keeping bees! This is because our wonderful bees provide 1 out of every 3 bites of food we eat. So, no bees means no food, and no us. Also, it is a well-known fact that bees are in trouble. Do you know that yearly losses of different honey bee colonies are now in the tens of thousands?

I know you will have a number of questions. For example, "Should I go for beekeeping? Maybe I should not. They won't survive in the city environment." Well, this is one of the most common myths that people have about beekeeping. It might surprise you, but 'beekeeping in cities' is becoming popular.

Actually, bees in towns are much healthier than the ones grown in the countryside. Also, they produce twice as much honey as bees in rural areas.

As urban beekeeping is becoming popular, it's a great idea for children to take up this hobby. If you would like to keep bees, this guide is for you.

Chapter 1
Bee-ing Ready and Understanding Bees

You know that knowledge is power. This is very true when you apply it to beginning beekeeping. You not only need knowledge but the right mix of knowledge. One of the most vital first steps in beekeeping is taking the time for some serious planning. As you have school, homework, and maybe boxing or viola lessons, you have to be realistic about your time and money.

The honey bee is one of several species of bee. It is the main part of the group of bees called social bees that often live in colonies. Here is something you may not know. All bees have five eyes. They have three simple eyes located on top of their head and two compound eyes. A standard hive contains about 60,000 bees.

A female bee is often a worker or a queen. Also, a single colony usually contains one queen and more than ten thousand workers. A worker bee lives for about 5-6 weeks in summers. You will know more as you go through this guide.

Endangered Species

Honey bees are slowly going extinct due to the heavy use of various pesticides in crops as well as specific blood-sucking parasites which reproduce only in bee colonies. This should concern us as out of the hundred different crop species that provide us with ninety percent of our food, almost 35 percent are pollinated by bees, bats, and birds. It is that simple.

Many countries throughout the world have seen a huge decline in the number of bee populations. Some of these regions include Brazil, China, North America, and Europe.

If you are like me and read the newspaper, you would know that the US government recently added the seven species of Hawaiian bees to the list of endangered bee species.
These are:
Hylaeus Anthracinus is also is known as an athricinan yellow-faced bee. This insect is mostly found in lowland forests and coastal areas. It looks beautiful.

Hylaeus Longiceps is widely known as a long head yellow-faced bee and has smoky-colored wings.

Hylaeus Assimulans is widespread to Hawaii; this is a yellow-faced bee and is relatively larger than other coastal bee species.

Hylaeus Facilis has a central face mark. This bee is also listed on the endangered bee species.

Hylaeus Hilaris is a coastal bee and has a reddish lower body with broad white lines. It looks very attractive.

Hylaeus Kuakea is small in size and has smoky black wings.

Hylaeus Mana is found in shrublands, wet forests, coastlines, lowland dry forests. This endangered bee has stretch marks on the face of females and narrow, broad lines on the lower body of male bees.

Pollinators, such as bees, have always been taken for granted. The good news is that we have finally realized that keeping bees and other pollinators alive is important for our economies.

All these seven species have a different appearance and live in different habitats. But one thing that is common in them is their declining number. To save these seven species of bees, central agencies are looking forward to providing funds. It will allow the bee populations to survive.

Bees and Their Contribution to Society

Do you know that bees carry the weight of the world on their tiny backs? Let me explain my friends what I mean. Bees are amazing creatures that deserve hearty thanks. This is because, without them, we would have ceased to exist quite a long time ago.

For starters, bees produce honey. Do you know that honey is the only insect created product that has many health benefits? Maybe your science teacher told you that!

Honey can help you sleep and treat sore throats and colds. After all, no one likes waking up in the morning with a sore throat, especially on a school day. Honey also strengthens the immune system and helps with treating minor skin conditions, burns and cuts.

Bees are also the most important pollinators. Bees are responsible for pollinating about 400 different crops and one-sixth of flowering plants. Isn't that awesome friends! I'll help you understand better, so let's dig a little deeper.

Pollination

We are all taught at a very young age that bees carry pollen from one plant to another and from one flower to another. This process is called pollination. You must have read about it in your science book. Whether you love to eat melons or apples, don't forget that plants require pollination to grow. Now, do you see how great these bees are!

Food Source

Bees produce honey for their colonies during winters. See how hardworking these tiny creatures are. Humans have been using honey for hundreds of thousands of years. We not only use honey as a sweet snack but also as a natural remedy.

And that is not all my friends. Critters, like opossums, raccoons, insects, and birds, love to eat honey.

Wild Plant Growth

And here is another fascinating thing about bees. Do you know that it is not only fruits and vegetables that depend on bees for pollination? Many wild plants depend on insect pollinators, like bees, to spread and grow. Many wild animals eat nuts, seeds, fruits, and berries and bees are responsible for their production as well. By the way, I love munching on fruits and berries also; just another reason to love bees.

Wax

I think you are familiar with beeswax candles; I even have a couple of them in my room. But do you know that beeswax has other uses too? For example, beeswax is present in beauty products, chewing gums, and lip balm, car wax and also used to waterproof leather.

So, we should not see bees as buzzing and loud pests that like to sting. Rather, we should thank them for the benefits they provide in the form of honey, sustaining important plant life and different food sources, and their great positive impact on many other animals.

Chapter 2:
Beekeepers Associations

Have you heard about beekeepers associations? Don't worry if you haven't, I'll explain. The main purpose of beekeepers' associations and clubs is to educate and support beekeepers, like you and I. If you are new to beekeeping, then joining a beekeepers' association or club will be advantageous for you.

Some of you might be wondering how other members would be. The good news is that generally, beekeepers are very friendly and social. They also love to discuss their work with other members. They love to talk about their hobbies. So, it is a great place to make new friends if you are into beekeeping.

More importantly, a bees' club is a great place to learn more about bees. Also, you get contact information and can build a strong network with other beekeepers in your neighborhood. So, whenever you face any problem with beekeeping, you can reach out to your club members.

Also, you will have all the updates about rules, regulations, and ordinance about beekeeping through your beekeeping association or club. And these organizations usually arrange fairs and events where members can sell their products. This will be a plus point for you. You will be able to sell your products at these events. Imagine earning money at such a young age!

Bees Association and Clubs

If you are interested in learning about bees' environment, and the art and science of beekeeping, bees associations and clubs are a perfect place for you to start. Here is a list of some bees associations and clubs in the U.S. Many of them have their own websites. You can check their websites for more details or information.

National-Regional Bees Associations and Clubs

- American Honey Producers Association
- Western Apicultural Society
- American Beekeeping Federation
- Eastern Apicultural Society
- Heartland Apicultural Society

Local Bees Associations and Clubs

- Allegheny Mountain Beekeepers Association (A.M.B.A.)
- Lehigh Valley Beekeepers Association
- Central Counties Beekeepers Association
- Beekeepers of Susquehanna Valley
- 2 Cs and a Bee Beekeepers' Association
- Bucks County Beekeepers Association
- Westmoreland County Beekeepers Association
- Monroe County Beekeepers Association
- Philadelphia Beekeepers Guild
- Beekeepers of ABCI (Armstrong, Butler, Clarion, and Indiana)
- Lackawanna Backyard Beekeepers
- Jefferson County Area Beekeepers Association
- Centre County Beekeepers Association
- Wayne County Beekeepers Association
- North Central PA Beekeepers Association
- Country Barn Farm Beekeeping Club
- Harriton House Beekeepers Association
- Washington County Beekeepers Association

Chapter 3:
Mentors

Do you know that most people (especially kids) are successful when they have a mentor to guide them? For example, you may have a sports mentor who you look up to. Whether you are on your school's basketball or football team, you know that a mentor can make a huge difference in improving your game. Well, my friends, the same is true in the case of beekeeping.

When you decide to become a beekeeper, you want to become the best one. Also, you want a happy, healthy, thriving, and productive hive.

Keep in mind that there are many things to consider when owning bees. Some of these things include pest control, creating an ideal environment for your bees, preparing them for winter, and much more. Do you think it will be difficult to handle? What if you find someone to help you along the way? A bee mentor can be a real help, especially if it is your first beehive.

Bee mentors have experience and knowledge. They know what to do and what not to do when keeping bees. Also, they can handle situations that may arise during beekeeping easily and efficiently. A bee mentor has connections with other beekeepers or suppliers. This can be a blessing as my uncle was to me whom introduced me into urban beekeeping.

Also, during your first beekeeping experience, you will have plenty of questions. I had quite a few questions. For example, can I keep my bees in a garden? What additional supplies should I use? Why is there a horde of bees outside the hive? A bee mentor will give answers to all your questions.

Finding a Beekeeping Mentor

Are you wondering where you can find a beekeeping mentor? I have you covered.

Local Beekeeping Club

If your city, town, or neighborhood has an active beekeeping club, it is your best bet for finding an excellent mentor. Note that local clubs often hold meetings monthly and discuss relevant topics as they relate to global and local issues. Beekeeping clubs are an ideal place to find active members that care about bees and also would like to see the next generation of beekeepers, like you, succeed.

Social Media

You must have a Facebook or Instagram account. You can use it to find a good mentor. As you get started with keeping bees, you should follow a couple of beekeepers on various social media sites, like Instagram, Facebook, and Twitter. More importantly, join a beekeeping group on Facebook. Then you can easily and quickly post that you are looking for a mentor and will be able to talk with many potential candidates before the meeting.

Chapter 4:
Language and Terms

Just like you need a dictionary when you are writing a book report on a classic literature novel, such as Lord of the Flies, you will need a list of terms used in beekeeping to understand things better.

It is very important that you understand and use proper terminology for beekeeping.

Keep in mind that asking questions with inappropriate words will only create confusion. Also, you may get an incorrect answer to your question. For this reason, you must know the terminologies that are commonly used in beekeeping.

1. **Abdomen**
The posterior (meaning toward the back) body part of a bee that contains the true stomach, honey stomach, reproductive organs, intestine, and sting.

2. **Apiary**
Also known as a bee yard, an apiary is a site where bee colonies are kept in hives by a beekeeper.

3. **Apiculture**
This is the art or practice of raising honey bees in a bee yard.

4. Apiology

Studying and understanding honey bees is called apiology. (The word sounds difficult, but it is very easy to understand)

5. Apis Mellifera

This is the scientific name of a honey bee commonly found in the United States.

6. Bearding

When honey bees gather on the front side of their hive to keep the temperature down in their nest, this practice is called bearding. Simple, isn't it? They usually do this during hot days or when their house is overcrowded with honey stores or bees.

7. Bee Bread

The food of honey bees made with a mix of pollen and nectar of honey. Nurse bees prepare this food for feeding the queen, drones, and larvae.

8. Beehive

It is a man-made box that contains movable frames. You are smart and know this term. Beehive is used to keep the colony of bees; one colony of bees in one hive.

9. Bee Space

It is a 6mm to 8mm space between hive parts and combs, which serves as a passage for bees. Honey bees use it to deposit propolis (a mixture used to seal open spaces in a hive). Also, they build extra combs in the gaps that are wider than 8mm.

10. Bees' Nest
Bees' nest is a place occupied by the bee colony. It is their habitat. Honey bees use the nest for two purposes; to raise young bees and to store food. Another simple term!

11. Beeswax or Bee Wax
A substance produced by worker bees with which honey bees build their combs. Bees produce small wax scales from their body.

12. Brood
Eggs, larvae, and pupae of honey bees are called brood. They are developing bees. They live in the brood box; it is the bottom box of a hive. To put it simply, they are young ones.

13. Brood Capping
When larvae are ready to lose pupae, the worker bees cover the cell with wax and bee hair; this is called brood capping.

14. Burr Comb
Burr comb is the small spaces in the frame where bees want to build a comb. Again very simple!

15. Cappings
It is a thin layer of bee wax that bees use to seal the cells of

ripe honey. Worker bees cover the cells to preserve the honey. It's just like we cover food.

16. Castes
Worker bees, queen, and drones are called castes.

17. Bees Colony
When worker bees, the queen, drones, and brood live together in a beehive, it is known as a bees colony. It is also called a bee family.

18. Comb
A comb is a sheet that consists of thousands of six-sided cells. Honey bees build the comb with beeswax. They use it to store pollen, brood, and honey.

19. Drawn Comb
Drawn combs are made from foundations frames, which the beekeeper inserts at the base of the hive. Worker bees draw comb on these frames with a depth of 12-15 mm.

20. Drone
Male bees have no sting. They have broader bodies than worker bees and have bigger eyes. Interestingly, drones do not perform any duties. In fact, they rely on worker bees for their food. The main purpose of drones is to make the virgin queen pregnant. They live in a drone comb, which has a larger cell than worker broods.

21. Eggs

The queen bee lays the eggs in cells. Fertilized eggs become the queen or workers. On the other hand, unfertilized eggs become drones.

22. Feral Bees

It is a colony of wild bees that are not kept by beekeepers; they live on their own. Feral bees do not live in hives. Instead, they build their nests in walls and trees, etc.

23. Frame

A frame is an object used to hold a wax comb. A frame usually consists of a top section, two sidebars, and a bottom section. Keep in mind that only framed hives use frames.

24. Framed Hive

It is a hive that contains individual sections of the colony's nest. A frame in this section of the beehive can be removed for inspection by the beekeeper. It is important to keep in mind here that these hives are very useful if you want to study the bees, brood, and eggs closely.

25. Hiving Bees

The process of installing a bee colony into a beehive is called hiving bees.

26. Hive body
Vertical beehives include a box that contains frames or top bars where bees build a comb.

27. Honey
A sweet substance that bees produce from the nectar

28. Honey Flow
It is a period when there is a plentiful supply of nectar for the bees to collect. It is a time during which abundant of honey is produced. It is also known as nectar flow.

29. Honey Sac
It is an organ located above the bee's stomach, like a kangaroo sack. Bees store the extracted nectar in their honey sac.

30. Larva
It is the second development stage of a bee; it appears as a white and legless insect.

31. Nectar
It is a fluid that bees collect from flowers and place into the cells of their comb. When the nectar is dehydrated, i.e., it loses water and becomes honey.

32. Nectar Dearth
It is the duration in which no nectar is available for bees to

extract from flowers.

33. Nest

A combination of wax combs in which honey bees live. Keep in mind that nests are not beehives.

34. Orienting

People often confuse this term with robbing or swarming. But orienting is the act when young bees come out of the hive to become familiar with the environment. Remember that frequent orienting is a sign of a healthy bee colony.

35. Pollen

Bees gather pollen from flowers to feed larvae. They store this powdery substance in comb cells that are stacked in brood boxes.

36. Propolis

Propolis is a mixture of resins used to seal open spaces in the hive. You will be surprised to know that propolis contains anti-bacterial properties that help protect the bee colony from the disease. Bees collect propolis from trees.

Chapter 5:
Neighbors and Nature

Consideration of Neighbors

We have to be good to our neighbors and don't cause them any inconvenience. When you start keeping bees, it will affect your neighbors. When you tell people, like your neighbors, you are a beekeeper, they would usually react in 2 ways – "That is so awesome, how did you get into beekeeping?" or they might not like it. Hopefully, if you're a young beekeeper, your neighbors would be of the first type.

In any case, it is up to you to take some steps to educate your neighbors and help them overcome their fears. Some things that you can easily do to put your neighbors at ease are discussed in the next section.

Position your beehive opening away from the neighbor's homes. As your bees would be coming and going frequently it is best to have them leaving the hive and flying towards your home and not the neighbor's home.

Bee-ing a Supportive Neighbor

You should restrict your bee yard to 2 hives or less. This is because having a few hives is much less intimidating to uneducated people than if you had several hives. Also, provide a nearby water source for your bees. That will keep them from collecting any water from your neighbor's pool and/or birdbath.

Use fences, hedges, or screens to alter the flight pattern of your bees. Do you know that bees keep a certain flight pattern when they leave and return to their hive? You can share this cool fact with your friends and neighbors. With a little planning you can alter that flight pattern. If you are a backyard beekeeper, you can build a screen or fence or plant a hedge close to the front of your hive. This will ensure that your bees fly high and steep when they take off and land.

Tell your neighbors that bees usually fly in about a 3-mile radius of home plate (about 6,000 acres). So, in most cases, they will visit a huge area which is not anywhere close to your neighbor's property.

People are often most excited about stuff they can benefit from, like I am excited about my Christmas presents in the holiday season. So, make it a habit to share a small jar of your fresh honey with your closest neighbors. Believe me when a young beekeeper brings over a tasty jar of honey it would put a smile on your neighbor's face.

Chapter 6:
Basic Tools

When you take up a new hobby you have to invest some money into it. For example, if you want to be a photographer, you will have to buy a camera. Similarly, you will need a few tools to get started with beekeeping.

The good news is that beekeeping tools aren't expensive. A few tools can help make your interactions with your bees much simpler, smoother, more exciting, and a lot safer.

1. Bee Suit

Your bee suit will be a great investment. You may buy cheaper bee suits and that's certainly okay when you are starting out. But, high-quality suits will give you more protection. You can even try a ventilated suit. It looks cool and your friend will love it.

2. The Bee Brush

It is an extremely soft bristled brush and you can use it to gently remove your bees from any honey supers, frames, or any another area where they might gather in your way. Obviously, how gentle the bee brush can be depends on how you use it.

3. Shoes

Beekeeping shoes are also important for keeping you safe. Again, my friends could you imagine digging your way through a beehive without having both your feet covered properly? So, you should use your boots when you are working with our bees.

4. Uncapping Tool

This is another important tool. If you would like to keep the honeycomb on a frame so your bees do not have to draw out new combs, you will need a way for uncapping the honeycomb. The good news is that an uncapping tool is inexpensive and will allow you to easily get just the caps off a comb.

You will find an uncapping fork as well as an uncapping knife. I prefer working with the uncapping fork.

5. Hive Tool

Often, bees like to seal the cracks in their hive with propolis. But don't worry as you can easily use the flat end of your hive tool in order to break the seal. Then once you are in the bee hive, you can scrape away excess comb.

These tools are inexpensive and worth buying rather than using something in the house.

6.Gloves

How can we forget gloves! You may use any work gloves for working with your bees, but in my opinion, leather ones are the best. Most beekeeper gloves on the market are leather for the hands and use fabric up to the elbows.

7.The Smoker

I think that of all the different tools in any beekeeper's shed, a smoker is easily the most used as well as the most iconic. Smoke is used for calming the bees so that you can easily get into their hive.

Note that the smoke helps mask the pheromones that your bees produce to communicate with one another. A smoker is great as it makes getting smoke very easy. You may use small twigs, wood chips, leaves, or even pine needles in your smoker. The smoker is usually made of top-grade stainless steel and has a solid chimney and strong metal guards to protect your hands.

8.Veil

Probably, a beekeeper's veil is the most vital piece of equipment you will use to stay safe. Keep in mind that even the gentlest bees could and will sting sometimes. Unfortunately, my friends we never know when that time can come.

Also, getting stung on your face or scalp is very painful; this is why a veil is very important. Also, like humans, bees are naturally curious, especially about small openings, like ears and nostrils.

Chapter 7:
Personal Equipment

Now my friends let's talk about personal beekeeping equipment that you will need as a beginner beekeeper. Are you excited? I am for sure!

1. Frames

Frames are essentially rectangles which hang inside the hive just like a filing system in your home. Your bees would make their comb inside these frames. Note that this is where your bees will make honey and lay brood. Now, you will have to decide if you only want to buy frames or buy plastic foundation as well.

Are you confused? Let me explain. The only difference is that if you purchase the foundation for your frames, it means less work for your bees, which means they will have more time to make honey.

2. Queen Catcher

This piece of equipment is handy when you would like to keep your queen separated from other bees for a while. A great example of this is when you're going through the hives. Often, it's easier to place the queen in this catcher to make sure you do not lose her in the process.

In my opinion, hair clip types are the best ones. This is because you can pick up the queen easily without hurting her. Your queen is precious!

3. Hive Stand

You would not want your bee hives on the ground. Note that they would be hard to lift and more importantly when your bee hives are on the ground, it is likely that various critters would mess with them. Now you don't want that, do you?

NEW VS. USED EQUIPMENT

For many new beekeepers used beekeeping equipment is very attractive. Seriously, don't you want to save some money? After all, we have a limited amount of pocket money. Buying used beekeeping equipment could save you plenty of money. But, it could also be costly in case you make too many mistakes.

The good news my fellow beekeepers is that you can easily avoid these mistakes. First of all, it is vital to ensure that you don't enable the spread of various diseases from your used bee keeping equipment, to the bees. Remember that there's a real risk of this happening, particularly with the bee hives as well as their components if you do not clean them properly.

Note that used hive tools and bee smokers are safer to use if they are cleaned properly. All you have to do is remove any propolis, wax, or other residues. I usually scorch all metallic surfaces with a blow torch. Then I dip them in a mixture of water and Clorox.

Some beekeeping equipment can be extremely difficult to clean. This is because of the nooks and crannies where viruses, mites, and other nasties may hide. In these circumstances, you should dispose of these items carefully.

If you are thinking about buying used beekeeping equipment, such as bee suit, bee hive, frames or jacket, consider the following tips and notes before you buy:

➢ You should not purchase any second-hand beekeeping equipment that can be hard to clean, like frames, because it would be hard to treat them to prevent the spread of diseases, viruses, and pests.

➢ You should ensure that all used beekeeping equipment and tools are safe and free from residues of wax, pollen, and honey. If you cannot clean them properly, then don't use them.

➢ You should buy new brushes. This is because it is hard to clean them, as they carry disease that may not be eradicated during your cleaning attempts.

➢ The most common kind of second-hand beekeeping equipment that is found for sale on the market is wooden ware. These are the parts of the hive. The good thing is that bottom boards, frames, supers, and inner and outer covers could last for many years. You will find most of these items for sale in early spring or fall.

Chapter 8:

Bee-Ginners Kit and Hive Set-up
Bee-ginning with One Hive

If you are a new beekeeper it is better to start small with one hive. You have two options; you can either build a beehive or buy one. If you build a bee hive, I highly suggest that you buy top bars as they are the most difficult part of a hive to make.

I will also recommend that you build your hive with a glass viewing window. Note that this is a great feature that you would not like to leave out. Want to know why? The window will allow you to see the progress of your bees without having to disturb their colony. Also, this gives you the chance to check on the bees anytime you would like.

The next decision is the placement of the hive. If you've a spot that gets early morning sun as well as a little shade in the afternoon, then it is perfect. If you live in a very warm climate, then you will probably like more afternoon shade.

What I love about bees is that they are very adaptable and awesome creatures and can often make nearly any location work provided there's water and food in the surrounding area.

You will also want to place the entrance of your bee hive away from any foot traffic. Note that less foot traffic at the hive's entrance the better it is for your bees, you as well as your friends.

PACKAGED BEES

One great way to start a new bee hive is by buying a package of bees that has a queen included. Packages are the most popular way to purchase bees. This is because they are the cheapest option and are easy to transport. These shipping boxes are available in different sizes that range from two to four pounds of worker bees.

These packages can be shipped via UPS or the post office; but, in case you live near the supplier, it's better to pick them up yourself. Note that packaged bees are often shipped with an average-sized can of sugar syrup in order to keep them fed and healthy until they are installed in your hive.

Here's good news my young beekeepers. Installation of packaged bees is very simple. You can spray a light sugary syrup on your bees through the screen. This will wet their wings and keep them from flying too much and make the process easier for you. Another great thing is that your bees would clean each other up quickly. I think that's great! They will also appreciate the tasty extra food to get their hive set up.

Now all you have to do is remove the syrup and shake the bees into the empty hive. You can use your parent or mentor's help, especially if it is your first time. Now you will have to suspend the queen in the package. The worker bees will be attracted to the queen. They will gather around the queen cage. And in a couple of days when things settle down, you can release the queen so she can start laying eggs.

I think the process is very simple. Do you agree?

BEST SEASON TO BEGIN BEEKEEPING

There is a suitable season for every activity. For example, spring is an ideal time for kids to play baseball or go horseback riding. But what is the best season of the year to begin beekeeping? When should kids, like you, do it?

Well, before I started, I had the same question and let me share with you what I've learned.

The best season to begin keeping bees in a majority of places is in spring. But, keep in mind that this may change a bit month by month, primarily depending on your specific climate zone. You should ideally try to start beekeeping when the rainy or cold season ends, and flowers begin to bloom. Note that bees start to get active in spring, but your spring preparation must be completed much earlier, most probably starting in autumn.

The best season to move the bees into the beehive also depends on where and what environment you happen to live in. In the US, for example, there is a variety of different climates between the West and East coast. I think you must have learned about it in your geography class.

The eastern states in the US experience humid and hot summers, and dry and cold winters. On the other hand, southwestern states often remain warm to hot throughout the year. In the tropics, things are different, and there's a wet and dry season instead of winter and summer.

I think that moving your bees to their beehive is an official start of your interesting, fun, and exciting beekeeping journey. And yes my fellow beekeepers, it is done often in spring.

WHEN TO ORDER BEES

This is another important question. You have to order the bees so that they can arrive by early spring. You have to keep in mind that ordering and receipt the bees are 2 different things. It is important to start ordering your bees around January or February so you can get them by early April. Depending on when they would arrive, you might have to feed your bees until May. After that, the bees will usually go outside their hives to find pollen for themselves.

You might be wondering why ordering your bees in January or February is important. I had the same question when I started beekeeping. The answer is very simple and easy to understand. People, who sell bees on the market, run out of stock very fast! As a result, if you order the bees in April or May, it may be a bit too late.

Chapter 9:
Queen, Drone, and Worker

Do you know that bees live in colonies like us? These colonies contain the queen bee, the drone, and worker bee. Also, the queen bee and worker bee are both female but note that only the queen can reproduce. Now you know why a queen is so important. On the other hand, all drones are male.

QUEEN

Each bee colony has just one queen. The queen's primary function is reproduction. This is because she is the only sexually developed female. Remember that queens lay the highest number of eggs in the spring as well as early summer.

Queen bees are the largest of all bees in a beehive. Do you know that she can lay about 1500 to 2000 eggs in a day? But, keep in mind that this does not happen every day. There are some days when the queen will not lay any eggs.

One queen can lay up to 250,000 eggs in a year and possibly over a million in her entire lifetime. Isn't that amazing! The only and important role of the queen is to mate and lay eggs. The queen is a little larger than the bees in the hive and has a longer abdomen as well. Her wings are shorter than the others. The wings of the queen cover about two-thirds (or 66 percent) of the length of her abdomen. Note that the queen has a longer stinger, but it has fewer barbs compared to those of the worker bees.

The queen bee can live for many years—sometimes for up to 5 years, but her average life span is two to three years. The queen bee only makes a single flight when she leaves her hive as a virgin queen. She does this to mate with any nearby drones. She spends the rest of her life inside the hive. This is because it is too risky for her to go outside the hive. Also, the queen is too important for the well-being of the colony. Another main function of a queen bee is producing pheromones.

About a week after coming out from the queen cell, the queen bee leaves the hive in order to mate with many drones in flight. Do you know that the queen bee mates usually in the afternoon? Here is another great fact. She mates with about seven to fifteen drones at a height of above 20 feet. Drones can find and recognize the queen bee by her special chemical odor (pheromone). Keep in mind that if poor weather conditions delay the queen's mating flight for over 20 days, she will lose the ability to mate.

After mating with drones, the queen returns to her hive and starts to lay eggs in about 48 hours. The colony's worker bees take care of the queen and fed her royal jelly. It is a tasty bee snack! Note that the number of eggs the queen bee lays depends on the quantity of food she gets. It also depends on the number of workers that can prepare beeswax cells for the eggs and care for the larva.

When old queens are accidentally lost, killed, or removed, the other bees in the hive choose younger worker larvae for producing emergency queens. Note that these queen bees are raised in worker cells.

DRONE

Drones are probably the laziest bees in a bee colony. They are like that one lazy friend we all have. And they just have one thing on their mind, which is to find a virgin queen bee to mate with! So, their only role, like queens, is to reproduce. Note that these male bees are much larger in size than worker bees. They also have bigger compound eyes with large and strong wings. They don't have any stinger.

Drones usually depend on workers for food, but they can easily feed themselves in the beehive after they're four days old. Do you know that drones eat 3 times as much food as other workers? This is why too many drones in the hive can place more pressure on the food supply of the colony.
Drones usually stay in the beehive until they're about eight

days old. And after that, they start to take orientation flights. They fly from the hive between noon and 4:00 p.m. in most cases. Drones do not take food from flowers.

The life of a drone is usually short but sweet. You will be surprised to know that their lifespan is just around three months. Also, note that if for any reason the food supply begins to get low, then worker bees kick the drones out of the beehive. This usually happens when bees prepare for winter, and the colony starts to slow down, and the food is too precious. Many drones die of starvation.

WORKERS

Worker bees are nonfertile females. This means they can't reproduce, like queen bees. Workers bees are also the busiest and most active bees in the hive! The worker bee often takes on several different important roles throughout her life. The tasks they perform depend on their age and maturity. The role of a worker bee is essential to the survival of a colony.

They polish and clean the cells, care for the queen, feed the brood, and remove debris. They also handle incoming nectar and guard the entrance, build beeswax combs, and ventilate and air-condition the bee hive during their first couple of weeks as adults. Later, they go out in the field and look for pollen, nectar, water, and propolis.

SPECIES

As a young beekeeper, one of the main questions you may have is, "What type of bees should I keep?" The good news is that there are several bees you can choose from, such as Carniolan, Italian, German, and Russian, bees, to name a few.

Italian Bees

They are the most popular bees in North American. These, like most commercial bees, are both gentle and great producers. Here is a small history fact for you. Italian bees were brought to the US in the mid-1800s. They are also considered the best bee species for beginning beekeepers. Italian bees use less propolis compared to some of the darker bees. These bees typically have bands on the abdomen with a brown or yellow color.

Here are some of the benefits of keeping Italian bees:
- ✓ Adaptable to various climates
- ✓ They are great honey producers
- ✓ Easy to manage
- ✓ Gentle and non-aggressive
- ✓ Large colonies
- ✓ Very hygienic
- ✓ Darker queen – which makes her easier to identify

Russian Bees

They are dark brown to black, but the yellow part of their abdomen is paler. Russian bees are comparatively new to North America and came to the US in 1997 from a region in Russia called Primorsky. Russian bees do well in cold climates. Russian bees are slightly more aggressive than other bees. But, this does not mean they will always sting. They often "head butt" instead of stinging potential threats. This is why they guard their hive carefully.

Here are some of the benefits of keeping Russian bees:
- ✓ They are not aggressive
- ✓ They do not consume a lot of honey
- ✓ Maintains queen bee cells all season long

Carniolan Bees

This is another important species of bee. Carniolan bees are a subtype of the western honeybee, and they are from Slovenia. Do you know that they can also be found in Romania, Hungary, Croatia, Herzegovina, Bosnia, and Serbia? They are dark brown in color and have brown spots on their abdomen. Here are some of the benefits of keeping Carniolan bees:
- ✓ They defend their hive effectively from various pests
- ✓ They are not aggressive towards beekeepers, so you will have a good time
- ✓ They can quickly adjust the size of their hives based on environmental factors

- ✓ They can store more honey, which means you will earn more money
- ✓ They are less likely to catch brood disease

Chapter 10:

Maintenance and Management
Personal Safety

I know that working with your bees can be a rewarding, exciting, and fun experience. But, there're a few risks! All young beekeepers should read the following information before working with their bees.

1. In the case of an emergency, please call 911; it can save someone's life.

2. When you are working with your bees, make sure that you bring another hive member with you. This will ensure that in the case of an emergency, you're not alone.

3. Working with your bees could be dangerous, so wear safety equipment to reduce the risk of something bad happening.

4. Do not wear any fragrances.

5. If a bee stings you:

   a. Remain calm
   b. Avoid any harsh and sudden movements
   c. Do not swat at your bees
   d. Step away from the bees slowly and leave the hive area
   e. Protect your eyes and face

HIVE PROTECTION

If you are already a young beekeeper, you will know the difference between your bees and pests and critters, like wasps. If you are wondering how you can protect your bees from vandals, wasps, and diseases (without getting stung), you have come to the right place.

Wasps, bugs, ants, and hornets can attack your beehive anytime, but particularly at or just before the honey harvest. This is when the smell of sweet and tasty honey is strong. And everyone loves honey, don't you?

You will also have to protect your beehive from the elements as your hive will be outside most of the time. These elements include rain and sleet.

Your beehive is at greater risk if it's:
- New
- Small
- Weak
- Battling mites and other pests

Here are some tips to protect your beehive:

USE BEEHIVE ROBBING SCREENS

Note that these screens protect your hive against wasps, pests, and robber bees. These newcomers may smell the honey, but will not be able to get inside your beehive through the screen. But your bees will figure out their way in to go and come as they please.

PAINT

Most beekeepers like to paint their beehives using a top quality exterior paint to protect them. You can use either latex or oil-based paints. And who does not like painting? It is so much fun. Also, go for semi-gloss paints as they are much easier and simpler to keep clean than other paints, like matte.

SHRINK YOUR BEEHIVE ENTRANCES

In case the robbing screen and paint do not work (or if they are not your thing), then you can easily make the entrances to your hive smaller. You can do it by adding tiny lumber pieces with wood glue.

Just as chokepoints are much easier and simpler to defend in battle (you can think of that amazing scene in The Lord of the Rings: Two Towers where they were trying to hold off the famous Uruk-hai at the Helm's Deep drawbridge). Similarly, a smaller beehive entrance is easier for bees to protect.

ELECTRIC FENCING

Do you know that bears also love honey? And bears can do serious damage to a beehive. So, what can you do as a beekeeper? In my opinion, one of the best ways to prevent bears from damaging the hives is to install electric net fencing. You can charge electric fences with batteries, solar energy, or electricity directly.

DISEASE PREVENTION TIPS

1. Regularly inspect the hive and look for dead larva in cells, discoloration on your bees and any strange odors.
2. Replace old hive parts after the outbreak. Replacing items, like frames, is a good way to ensure that you get rid of any spores that may cause infection.
3. Keep your beehive ventilated. This will prevent the growth of spores.
4. Don't feed any untreated honey products to your bees as they might contain fungi or bacteria.

About the Author

Born February 18, 2007 in Lexington, KY and raised in Louisville, KY - home of Muhammad Ali, the greatest boxer and humanitarian of all time who coined the phrase, "Float like a butterfly, sting like a bee" Keith was given the nickname "Little Muddiez" by his father, referencing the Bible teaching of God's formation of man from the mud and clay of the earth, endowing man with the divine instruction to "have dominion over the fish of the sea, over the birds of the air and over every living creature that roams the earth."

From the time Keith could crawl, he had an interest in music and instruments, as well as sports; but nothing could compare to his infatuation with nature. Before he could walk, Keith would sometimes crawl across the family room floor to the dog cage, pulling himself erect on the side of the cage, and then reaching his entire arm between the bars just to pet the puppies and tug on their floppy ears.

Keith would gaze at his fish tank for hours as a toddler, somehow convincing his parents to pick him up to allow him to stick his hands - and sometimes toes - inside the tank just to be closer to the fish, turtles, and hermit crabs. Over the years at one time or another, he would have had practically every pet known to man. Zoos, aquariums, farm field trips, and family nature walks were among his favorite excursions.

Suddenly in 2017, due to his parents' incarceration, Keith found himself experiencing the trauma of living in a world without either parent being present or part of his everyday life. Eventually, he began to fail every subject in school, had to move between two grandmothers' and two uncles' homes, and was sent to numerous mental health specialist to try to address his growing psychological issues. It reached a point where only divine intervention would be able to snap the chain which linked him to what some call the "generational curse," which impacts many lower-income and urban youth.

One morning, while staying with his uncle, Keith was tossed an oversized beekeeper's suit and instructed to put it on, then taken to the backyard where he witnessed his first hive and swarm. Immediately inspired and reconnected to his love of nature for the first time in months, peace, at last, superseded his struggles, anxieties, doubts, and misfortunes. Diligent observation of the honey bees began to open his eyes to the queen bee's role and importance to her hive just as his mother and grandmothers are the foundation and key to his own family's survival. Worker bees helped him appreciate community and unity both inside and outside of the home by demonstrating love, strength, and protection.

Able to process vast amounts of information at an early age by utilizing the power of thought, Keith birthed the idea to help bring awareness to others of the correlation and significance of beekeeping, community, unity, nature and the many contributions of bees to the cycle of life and humanity, while being an advocate of what we call "Mental Health Miracles."

Beekeeping can be therapeutic for people with mental health issues, such as depression, anxiety and trauma. When taking part in beekeeping as a group, people are delighted to be part of a team and appreciate the social skills they gain in the process.

Some patients state that when they care for bees they have a sense of purpose, which gives them fulfillment and helps them take their mind off of things and Keith is one good example.

Today Keith has been reunited with his mother and regularly communicates with his father. He has played the piano and viola in numerous musical recitals throughout Kentucky. He is now passing all classes and is doing well in school. He is the captain of his basketball team and also an amateur boxer who loves Muhammad Ali.

He has attended numerous beekeeping seminars and workshops. Keith is currently working with his family in establishing a charitable and volunteer-based organization which would take on the responsibility of providing resources, information, and education activities that directly reunites our youth with nature and allows for the development of healthy social, interpersonal, ecological, and professional skills while providing an alternative solution to various mental health challenges.

For more information, donations or to share your own personal "Mental Health Miracle" with others contact us at:

Website:
Beeing2gether.com

Email:
Beeing2gether@gmail.com

Address:
3131 Crums Lane
Suite #16891
Louisville, KY 40256

Keith A. Griffith III

Made in the USA
Monee, IL
24 July 2020